The Mind Of A Maniac

A Window To The Soul

Brian Umstattd

BookLeaf Publishing

India | USA | UK

Made with ❤ on the BookLeaf Publishing Platform
www.bookleafpub.in
www.bookleafpub.com

Dedication

To my children and loving wife.

Preface

In this book, I aim to show merely words, some of wisdom, some of despair, and others of self reflection. This book is intended to be nothing more than poetic manifestation of chaotic minds.

Acknowledgements

I would like to acknowledge my past present a future self. I want to thank every long day, every lonely night, and every moment in between.

1. Your Touch

Light the match,
We've got a love like fire.
Ill swallow the flames,
You are my one desire.
Too hot to touch,
Gasoline makes our love burn brighter.

I've got a habit,
Baby it is you.
It is in everything you say,
It is in everything you do.
I can't get enough
Baby, you're all that I pursue

2. Shattered Glass

Let the blood spill to the floor and paint a masterpiece of
sorrow.
I don't know my reflection,
I see myself through the shattered glass, shards broken
like a pice of shattered mirror.
Shadows dance upon these walls, whispering tales of
grief.
Each drop of anguish falls, waving a tapestry of disbelief.

In this hall of fractured dreams, I search for a way to
mend,
the shards of my shattered soul, the pieces of a friend.
Like the glass that lies in shards, my heart remains
unhole,
A reflection of the pains, that cannot be untold.

Through these shards of shattered glass, I can see my
ghostly face,
It serves as a reminder of what I cannot erase.
With the blood that spilled onto the floor, a constant

reminder stays,

Of the beauty that was lost, in the shattered remains of yesterdays.

3. Shadows

In the abyss, where's the shadows feast,
Dwells sorrow, the ceaseless beast.
Blood-stained tears and silent screams,
Life's twisted broken dreams.

Where there is no dawn, no lights, just endless night
There is a void, where souls forever fight.
Their bones are shattered and their hopes erased,
In the depths of infinity, in this wretched and cursed
place.

Silence cries, as the darkness swells.
Listen to the symphony of private hells.
Lost in grief, there's no path to trace,
Lies eternal torment to which there's no escape.

Yet in this darkness, a spark remains,
Like a whisper of light through the endless pains.
One's hope is reborn, like a glimmering flame,
The fire inside guides their souls to rise again.

Their dreams are fleeting and the shadows mock.
Promises broke, like a brittle rock.
See even hope's light can fade away,
In this land where nightmares play.

From this despair, a new strength grows,
Through the darkness its light shows.
Resilience shines, like a guiding star,
The flames of fire remind us who we are.

4. Depths of My Soul

In the moon's glow, we danced as one.
Underneath the stars, our journey's long begun.
You and I were made together.
You and I were made to see forever.

In my sight, a tree stands tall,
Whispering a reminder, should our love ever fall.
Life's branches would be bare, without guiding light.
Without you shadows would embrace the night.

In the depths of my soul, a storms will rage.
From the sins I have committed, on life's little stage.
In her living eyes, a mystery unfolds.
Why she dances with me, the sinner she holds.

On life's grand stage, we all take our part.
The best the ever told, is love's bleeding heart.
Through the highs and the lows, we all have our roles.
The greatest story, is love that consoles.

5. A Web of Deceit

In a web of deceit, the fly is ensnared,
By the spider's wickedness, unprepared.
Each silky thread, a twisted tale.
The fly's innocence begins to pale.

With every falsehood that the spider weaves,
The fly's trust slowly and painfully cleaves.
Deep within, a flicker of doubt.
The fly yearns for freedom, she lets out a shout.

For truth is a beacon, it shines bright.
Guiding the fly, through the darkest of night.
With courage and strength, it will again rise.
Breaking free from the web of deceit and the lies.

Let the spider spin its deceit,
the flys spirit won't accept defeat.
In the end, the truth shall conquer it all,
The fly shall rise, forever stand tall.

6. Tears of Love

Those that I love, they don't hear my cries.
They say the day you're loved the most, is when anyone
dies.
I just can't seem to find reason,
I am so tired of fighting, I don't even want to try.

A child without vision, a boy without a dream,
Turned into a man, with low self esteem.
Hiding in my own shadows, I don't want to be seen.
hiding in the game of my shame, the devils scheme.

Money comes, and money goes.
The root of all evil, it's always been the people.
Humanity lost, before i found myself.
I tasted the sweet nectar of sin, a sin that is lethal.

7. Phoenix

I'm not new to the fire
Phoenix born in the flame.
Peace in my nest, when laid to death,
Rebirth, Renewed, with the same name.

I'm not afraid of the heat,
I will sore the amber sky.
Risen from the ashes,
Hear me when I sing my melodic cry.

The immortal red Son
Dead risen, resurrection
Prince of peace in my heart,
Images of creation.

Until infinity
Before time began.
New hope, new night, new day.
Watch as these demons run away.

Rapture surely coming swiftly,
Apocalypse is now
In the destruction of ones self
Ending all worldly desire

The city of the moon
Jerichos walls came down
River jordan, crossing,
God's trumpets blowing through the town.

Sins washed by the hands of blood
A lamb led to slaughter
Saved from deaths violent sting
You me, his son and daughter.

8. Tick Tock

Tick Tick Tock, goes the hands of a clock,
Of time, while the world is spinning,
Too loud and too fast,
Too furious to make sense of the noise.
Inside my mind, I've lost my Spirit,
Have you seen it?

Tick, tick, no tock, as the hands of time are frozen like,
Jack, bury me with a Rose,
By a different name, call her anxiety.
Disorder, chaos, call her a restless soul.
She's trained to mislead you, guide you into the dark,
Dark side of the moon, I've lost my spirit.
Have you seen it?

Tick Tick, the hands stay stuck
In the middle with the pressure of fulfilling,
Prophecy, eye for an eye, such poetic justice,
Conforming to the laws of America,
The beautiful spiral into the depths of hell,

Oh can you hear me cry from the other side,
How long will I slide, I've lost my spirit.
Have you seen it?

9. Jesus Rose

I was gone for a little bit, but now I am back.
Jesus died, Jesus rose, Jesus came to get me on track.
I went away, I lost my sight, I ran so far, I went astray.
I've got my vision, I can see, Jesus Christ was here to
stay.
The prodigal Son, he knew the places that I had been.
Jesus came and washed away my sin.
Just to chase the one, Jesus left the 99.
Out of the shadows, I came out of the dark, time to let
my Spirit shine.
He gave me life, he defeated death.
He gave me hope, mercy he gave me breathe.
As he conquered the world, He is the one.
On the cross he died, not before he said it is done!

10. Forgiven

Am I forgiven,

Am I so blessed?

Am I forgiven,

Can I forget all the rest?

Will I see the Heavens,

Did I pass the test?

Am I forgiven,

For the times I wanted my way?

Am I forgiven by the almighty Yahweh?

When I get to the Heavens,

Well done my son, will he say?

Am I forgiven,

By the savior who knows where I've been?

I am forgiven

And I am forgiven,

I've got a Savior to defeat all of my sin!

11. Unholy Water

I was baptized, in the Devils unholy water.
Fighting for my Soul, the river spills on everything in
sight.
Unholy waters, it was just a little wetter, it was just a
little hotter.
I was baptized in the heat, baptized in the fire.
We sell or Soul for a dollar, just to get what we desire.
Baptized in the mud, always running from myself.
Always chasing the white rabbit, fast tracking chasing
death.
Just a little quicker, I must go a little faster.
I was baptized int he dark, I got baptized in the bloody
river.
All it cost me was my freedom, I never knew would be
my master.

12. The Story of a Shadow

My shadow tells a story of the places I have been.
Through the long night, to the lonely mornings,
I am a broken soul, caution getting close, this is the only
warning.
My shadow tells a story of a life full of sin,
My shadow tells a story, this is the end.

My shadow tells a story, of a man in darkness.
Through the empty bottles, laying on the floor with
cigarettes in a tray.
I am a broken soul, caution getting close, listen when I
say.
My shadow tells a story, of a man made heartless.
My shadow tells a story of the devil, my lone accomplice.

My shadow tells a story of a man given up on life.
Through the troubles of my own made by my own hand.
Im a broken man, pay head, please understand.
My shadow tells a story of the chaos in the mind.

My shadow tells a story, of a man lost, one you cannot find.

13. If I were the Devil

Caffeine, nicotine, doesn't matter, anything.
Caffeine, nicotine, anything, anything, just to ease the
sting.
If i were the Devil, I'll tell you what I'd do.
I'd conjure up a story, and tell it just to you.
And if I were the Devil, let me tell you what I'd do.
I'd confuse the world and would hide what is true.

Caffeine, nicotine, all of the chemicals hit your brain.
If I were the Devil, let me tell you what I'd do.
Id make you lose yourself and make you go insane.

Caffeine, nicotine, anything, anything, anything to ease
my mind.
If I were the Devil, let me tell you what I'd do.
if i were the Devil, I'd steal your sight from the grace in
the world, id make you go blind.

14. Haiku

Smoke covers the sky
Enthralled by the fire of life
No water in sight

Run as the bridges burn
Feel the fires heat on your neck
No turning back now

Deafening silence
Overwhelming isolation
Peace squandered by scorn

Reignite the flame
Her exhilarating touch

A man senses peace

A lit cigarette
Down a never ending road
Hearts no longer burn

Shining in darkness
Illuminating the heart
Stars in the night sky

My brown eyed lover
Cherished like memories old
Illuminating

Rivers
Raging so calm
Contradictions move mountains
Flowing untamed, wild, gently
Patient

15. Split

Living in heaven
These walls are melting in hell
Angels surround me
But they're only here when I am well.

Sleeping in a gutter
But I feel like I'm equal to God
Demons all around me, they make me their friend
Fortune tells me they'll be here in the end.

Bright lights and good spirits
Can't seem to save my soul
I see no way out from here
When 'm trapped in the bottomless hole.

Schizophrenic Psycho
Bi-Polar Mind
Obsessions of the heart
Too scared to look inside, too scared of what I'll find

Trapped inside all of my life
With no one but my inner voice
The only comfort I have ever known
In my DNA, I never really had a choice.

Say goodbye to my only love
Break his heart and let him go
Let him stay and have no peace
Let him stay and feel so low

Frightened and erratic child
Manic episode, I can feel it coming
Adrenaline is flowing
Mind starts racing, the horses are running.

Bloods rushes
I can feel it, it's so warm
Electrifying sensations
Lightening in the storm.

Heavy depression, I'm so lonely and tired
The weight of the waves are crashing into the shore
Left here alone on a desolate island
Desperately I don't want to be here much more.

Sinking and th drowning begins
The water has risen its above my neck

I reach for those angels--abandoned again
My demons arrive, they're here just to check.

Balanced behavior
Manage the outcome
Can't change my mind
Best to remain numb.

Vigilant battle
A never ending war
A new fight tomorrow
Let's see what's in store.

16. Two Are One

In the depths of my mind, two narratives intertwine.
One whispers of darkness, the other seeks to shine.
A battle within, just a tale of strife and redemption.
A journey through addiction, seeking life's one
exemption.

Oh, I have walked the path of the shadows, I have fought
the demons, that are so fierce.
I have found the strength within, to overcome and
persevere.
Through the highs and the lows, I have learned to rise
above.
A story of triumph and life full of love.

Adventure calls, like a fire in my soul.
From mountain peaks to raging rivers, I dare to be bold.
I have climbed the highest peaks, felt the rush of the
wind.
I have expired uncharted territories, where few have
been.

Oh, I have danced with danger, embraced the thrill of the
unknown.
Living life to its fullest, spirit brightly shown.
Through the twists and the turns, I have found my way.
An adventurers spirit, guiding each day.

In the midst of it all, come a greater purpose.
To be a father, a guiding light, a love that is endless.
Every step that I take, I now try to be an example,
To teach, and to nurture, the chains I dismantle.

I have faced my demons and embraced the call of the
wild,
But my greatest adventure, is a father to a child.
through the highs and the lows, Ive risen above,
A story of triumph a life filled with love.

So let the melodies, of my life, be heard
A symphony of strength, adventure and love
They are interwoven in every word.
I've overcome my addiction, embraced with dear of
unknown.
I have finally found a love that's truly grown.

17. Lost at Sea

In a world where the shadows play,
A battle rages night and day.
Different faces, different names,
Inside my mind, constant games.

I am lost in a sea of identities,
Caught in a storm of complexities.
Each personality, a piece of me,
Yearning for unity, longing to be free.

One moment I'm strong, confident and bold.
The next fragile and lost, feeling so cold.
A kaleidoscope of thoughts and emotions,
Navigating a maze of inner oceans.

I am lost in the seas of identity,
Caught in a ström of complexity,
Each personality a piece of me,
Yearning for unity, longing to be set free

Amidst the chaos, I will find my way,
Discovering strength with each passing day.
Embracing fragments, finding common ground.
A symphony of selves, harmoniously bound.

Im in a sea full of identities,
Caught in a storm of complexities
Each personality a piece of me
Yearning for unity, longing to be set free.

Though the struggle may be hard to bear,
I'll embrace my differences and show I care.
For deep within this intricate design,
I find acceptance and peace of mind.

18. Whirlwind

In the whirlwind of my mind, a hurricane of thoughts,
Bipolar mania, a wild ride that can't be caught.
Colors vibrant, energy soars high,
Deep inside, a storm I cannot deny.

Oh, bipolar mind, you're a double edged sword,
Filling me with fire, but leaving me untoward.
Through the highs and the lows, I always find my way,
Navigating the roller coaster that is day by day.

Creativity bursts, like fireworks in the night,
Ideas racing, burning bright with might.
Amidst the chaos, I search for the calm,
A balance within, a soothing healing balm.

Bipolar mind, a double edged sword,
Filling me with fire, but leaving me untoward.
Through the highs and the lows, I find my way,
Navigating this rollercoaster, day by day.

Friends and loved one, always by my side,
Support and understanding, my gentle guide.
Together we face the challenges we find,
Embracing the complexities, of my mind.

Bi polar mind, you're a double edged sword,
Filling me with fire, leaving me untoward.
Through the highs and the lows, I always find my way,
Navigating this rollercoaster, every single day.

In the depths of this journey, I learn and I grow,
Discovering strength, I never knew that I'd know.
Bipolar mind, only a part of who I am,
I'll face it head on, rise above, solid ground I will stand.

19. Tiggered

Trigger, trigger, trigger,
Living inside a phone,
Tik Tok, Facebook, snapchat all alone.
Zombies now, we have no mind of our own.

CapCut, filters, anything to hide our face.
Show them whatever you want, this isn't myspace.
Hide and seek, big foot log off you chameleon,
Cover up, make up, masks on, veiled in lace.

YouTube trained, social media lies.
Flas, flash, flash
The neons straining our eyes.
The hungry wolf, at the sheep, he wore no disguise.

Insta, insta, instant gratification
More, more, more
Dopamine rushes, serotonin flows, electric sensations.
Hollywood dreams, late night scenes, californication

Follow, subscribe, thumbs up if you like me.
Smoke, smoke, smoke on my phone screen.
Track stars, running all that we see
Masterminds, until they become your personality.

Trapped in our own world, everything that we made it
Not a thing out of place, not even a little bit.
Click, click, photoshop, we're made in our own image,
Did you make a symphony, or are you living in a pit.

Rumble, rumble, rumble
Tweety birds chirping in the jungle.
Cancel culture vultures, you're going to be in trouble.
Bitcoin, inflation, the animals live in a bubble.

Taste the nectar, the sweet sip of the curse.
Out of touch with reality, always choosing what's worse.
Simulated, simulator, living in a simulation.
Robotic, you're living in the meta verse.

Can't you see, can't you see, what i want you to see.
You're here for eternity, no table for two.
Linked in, plugged out, no clue who you are.
Step out of the system, you don't have to go far.

20. Bad Tattoos

I've got a couple of bad tattoos,
A couple of screws loose,
I've got a bad attitude,
when I don't know what to do.
I spend all of my nights,
Just trying to forget about you.
In a bottle full of whiskey'And a bottle full of pills.
A couple of swishers full of memories,
And all the lies i thought were true.
I've got a little bit of bad news,
A little bit of I can't lose.
I've got a little bit of old blue,
When I think about the good times
Spending all of my days
Just trying to forget about you.
In a cell of my own,
A prison in my mind.
I'd do anything together out of here,
Smelling all of the white lines,
It's the best way to stop a heart...ache

There's been too much to take.
If you love me, let me fly,
Let me settle, let this be my last goodbye.

21. Secrets

I told you my secrets
Never meant to be told
Keep them locked away
Hold on to them until we are old

I told you my secrets
Now they won't let me go
Meant to stay silent, these demons
Only you and me know

Used them for pleasure
You used them for gain
Used them for anger
You used them for pain

Prayed on my weakness
Monsters returned
Deceitful flames reignited
Hateful spirits you invited

www.ingramcontent.com/pod-product-compliance
Lightning Source LLC
LaVergne TN
LVHW010924200726

843509LV00013B/2056